# OVER THE TOP

First published in Great Britain by
KEVIN MAYHEW LTD
Rattlesden
Bury St Edmunds
Suffolk IP30 0SZ

ISBN 0-86209-107-1



Cover design by Rob Williams
Music origination by MSS Studios, Cae Deintur, Dolgellau, Gwynedd
Printed and bound in Great Britain by J.B. Offset (Marks Tey) Ltd., Colchester, Essex

# CONTENTS

**CHRISTOPHER GOWER** is Organist and Master of the Choristers at Peterborough Cathedral. Before his present appointment, he was Organist and Master of the Choristers at Portsmouth Cathedral, and Organ Scholar at Magdalene College, Oxford, where he studied with Dr Bernard Rose.

# As with Gladness Men of Old

Dix 77.77.77.

From a chorale by C. Kocher 1786-1872
Abridged by W. H. Monk 1823-89

1. As with glad - ness men of old did the gui - ding star be - hold,
2. As with joy - ful steps they sped to that low - ly man - ger - bed,
3. As they of - fered gifts most rare at that man - ger rude and bare,
4. Ho - ly Je - su, ev - ry day keep us in the nar - row way;
as with joy they hailed its light, lead - ing on - ward, beam - ing bright,
there to bend the knee be - fore him whom heaven and earth a - dore,
so may we with ho - ly joy, pure, and free from sin's al - loy,
and, when earth - ly things are past, bring our ran - somed souls at last
so, most grad - cious God, may we ev - er - more be led to thee.
so may we with will - ing feet ev - er seek thy mer - cy seat.
all our cost - liest trea - sures bring, Christ to thee our heaven - ly King.
where they need no star to guide, where no clouds thy glo - ry hide.

DESCANT
Descant by Christopher Gower
5. In the heav' - nly coun - try bright need they no cre - a - ted light;
ALL VOICES
5. In the heav' - nly coun - try bright need they no cre - a - ted light;
then its Light, its Joy, its Crown, thou its Sun which goes not down:
then its Light, its Joy, its Crown, thou its Sun which goes not down:
there-fore ev - er may we sing Al - le - lu - ias to our King.
there - fore ev - er may we sing Al - le - lu - ias to our King.

W. Chatterton Dix, 1837-1898

# Be Thou My Guardian and My Guide

Abridge CM.

Isaac Smith(d.1805)

1. Be thou my guar - dian and my guide, and
2. The world, the flesh, and Sa - tan dwell a -
3. And if I temp - ted am to sin, and
hear me when I call; let not my slip - p'ry
round the path I tread; O save me from the
out - ward things are strong, do thou, O Lord, keep
foot - steps slide, and hold me lest I fall.
snares of hell, thou quick - 'ner of the dead.
watch with - in, and save my soul from wrong.

Descant by Christopher Gower
DESCANT
4. Still let me ever watch and pray; and feel that I am frail; that if the tempter cross my way, yet he may not pre - vail.
ALL VOICES
4. Still let me ev - er watch and pray; and feel that I am frail; that if the temp - ter cross my way, yet he may not pre - vail.

Isaac Williams 1802-1865

# Christ is Made the Sure Foundation

Westminster Abbey 87.87.87.

Adapted from the *Alleluias* in Purcell's 'O God, Thou art my God' for BELVILLE in *The Psalmist* 1843

1. Christ is made the sure found - a - tion,
2. All that de - di - ca - ted Ci - ty,
3. To this tem - ple, where we call thee,
4. Here vouch - safe to all thy ser - vants
and the pre - - cious cor - ner - - stone,
dear - ly loved by God on high,
come, O Lord of Hosts, to - - day;
what they sup - - pli - cate to gain;
who the two walls un - - der - ly - ing,
in ex - ul - tant ju - - bi - la - tion
with thy won - ted lov - - ing kind - ness
here to have and hold for ev - er
bound in each, binds both in one,
pours per - pet - ual mel - o - dy:
hear thy peo - ple as they pray;
those good things their prayers ob - tain,

ho - ly Si - on's help for ev - er,
God the One, and God the Tri - nal,
and thy full - est ben - e - dic - tion
and here - af - ter in thy glo - ry
and her con - fi - dence a - lone.
sing - ing ev - er - last - ing - ly.
shed with - in its walls for ay.
with thy bless - ed ones to reign.

Descant by Christopher Gower

DESCANT
5. Laud and hon - our to the Fa - ther;
ALL VOICES
5. Laud and hon - our to the Fa - ther;
laud and hon - our to the Son; laud and hon -
laud and hon - our to the Son; laud and
our to the Spi - rit; ev - er Three and
hon - our to the Spi - rit; ev - er Three and

ev - er One, con - sub - stan - tial, co - et -
ev - er One, con - sub - stan - tial, co - et -
- er - nal, while un - end - ing a - - ges run.
- er - nal, while un - end - ing a - - ges run.

Latin, c. 7th century
Tr. J. M. Neale 1818-1866

# Christ the Lord is Risen Again

Würtemburg 77.77. Alleluia

Later form of a melody in *Hundert Arien* Dresden 1694 adapted by W. H. Monk 1823-89

1. Christ the Lord is risen a - gain, Christ hath bro - ken ev - 'ry chain. Hark, an - gel - ic voi - ces cry, sing - ing ev - er - more on high.
2. He who gave for us his life, who for us en - dured the strife, is our Pas - chal Lamb to - day! We too sing for joy, and say
3. He who bore all pain and loss com - fort - less up - on the cross, lives in glo - ry now on high, pleads for us, and hears our cry.
4. He whose path no re - cords tell, who des-cend - ed in - to hell; who the strong man armed hath bound, now in high - est heaven is crowned.
5. Now he bids us tell a - broad how the lost may be re - stored, how the pen - i - tent for - given, how we too may en - ter heaven.
Al - - le - lu - ia!

Descant by Christopher Gower

DESCANT
6. Thou, our Pas - chal Lamb in - deed, Christ to - day thy peo - ple feed; take our
ALL VOICES
6. Thou, our Pas - chal Lamb in - deed, Christ, to - day thy peo - ple feed; take our sins and
sins a - way that we all may sing for ay, Al - - - le - lu - ia.
guilt a - way, that we all may sing for ay, Al - - - le - lu - ia.

German, Michael Weisse c. 1480-1534
Tr. Catherine Winkworth 1827-1878

# Come, Ye Faithful, Raise the Anthem

Neander 87.87.87.

Melody set to *Unser Herrscher* in *Alpha und Omega* by Joachim Neander 1640-80

1. Come, ye faith - ful, raise the an - them cleave the skies with shouts of praise;
2. Ere he raised the lof - ty moun - tains, formed the sea, or built the sky,
3. Now on those e - ter - nal moun - tains stands the sap - phire throne, all bright,
4. Bring your harps. and bring your in - cense, sweep the string and pour the lay;
sing to him who found the ran - som, an - cient of e - ter - nal days,
love e - ter - nal, free, and bound - less, forced the Lord of life to die,
with the cease - less al - le - lu - yas which they raise, the sons of light;
let the earth pro - claim his won - ders, king of that ce - les - tial day;
God e - ter - nal, word in - car - nate whom the heaven of heaven o - beys.
lift - ed up the Prince of prin - ces on the throne of Cal - va - ry.
Si - on's peo - ple tell his prais - es, vic - tor af - ter hard - won fight.
he the Lamb once slain is wor - thy, who was dead, and lives for ay.

Descant by Christopher Gower

DESCANT
5. Laud and hon-our to the Fa - ther, Laud and hon - our to the Son, Laud and
ALL VOICES
5. Laud and hon - our to the Fa - ther, Laud and hon - our to the Son,
hon - - - our to the Spi - rit, ev-er Three and ev - er One, One in
Laud and hon - our to the Spi - rit, ev - er Three and ev - er One,
love and one in splen - dour while un-end - ing ag - es run.
One in love and One in splen - dour while un-end - ing ag - es run.

Job Hupton 1762-1849 and J.M.Neale 1818-1866

# Forth in thy Name, O Lord, I Go

Song 34 (Angels' Song) LM

Melody and bass by
Orlando Gibbons 1583-1625

1. Forth in thy name, O Lord, I go, my dai - ly lab - our to pur - sue; thee, on - ly thee, re-solved to know, in all I think or speak or do.
2. The task thy wis - dom hath as - signed O let me cheer - ful - ly ful - fil; in all my works thy pres - ence find, and prove thy good and per-fect will.
3. Pre - serve me from my cal - ling's snare, and hide my sim - ple heart a - bove, a - bove the thorns of chock-ing care, the gild - ed baits of world-ly love.
4. Thee may I set at my right hand, whose eyes my in - most sub - stance see, and la - bour on at thy com-mand, and of - fer all my works to thee.
5. Give me to bear thy ea - sy yoke, and ev - 'ry mo - ment watch and pray, and still to things e - ter - nal look, and has - ten to thy glo-rious day;

Descant by Christopher Gower

DESCANT
5. For thee de - light - ful - ly em - ploy, what e'er thy boun - teous grace hath
ALL VOICES
5. For thee de - light - ful - ly em - ploy, what e'er thy boun - teous grace hath
giv'n, and run my course with ev - en joy, and close-ly walk with thee to heav'n.
given, and run my course with ev - en joy, and close-ly walk with thee to heav'n.

Charles Wesley 1707-1788

# In the Bleak Mid-Winter

Gustav Holst 1873-1934

Cranham Irregular

1. In the bleak mid – win - ter fros - ty wind made moan,
2. Our God, heaven can - not hold him nor earth sus - tain;
3. E - nough for him, whom Chur - u - bim wor - ship night and day, A
4. An - gels and arch - an - gels may have ga - thered there,
earth stood hard as i - - ron, wa - ter like a stone:
heaven and earth shall flee a - way when he comes to reign.
breast - full of milk, and a man - ger - ful of hay: E -
Cher - u - bim and ser - a - phim throng - ed the air but
snow had fall - en, snow on snow, snow on snow,
In the bleak mid - win - - ter a sta - ble place suf - ficed the
nough for him, whom an - - gels fall down be - fore, the
on - ly his mo - - ther in her mai - den bliss
in the bleak mid - win - ter, long a - go.
Lord God Al - migh - ty, Je - sus Christ.
ox and ass and ca - mel which a - dore.
wor - shipped the be - lov - ed with a kiss.

Descant by Christopher Gower
DESCANT
5. What can I give him, poor as I am? If I were a shep - herd I would bring a lamb; if I were a wise man I would do my part; yet what I can I give him, give my heart.
ALL VOICES
5. What can I give him, poor as I am? If I were a shep - herd I would bring a lamb; if I were a wise man I would do my part; yet what I can I give him, give my heart.

Christina Rossetti 1830-1894

# Jesus Christ is Risen Today

Easter Hymn 77.77. & Alleluias

from 'Lyra Davidica' 1708

1. Je - sus Christ is ris'n to - day, al - - - - - - le - lu - ia,
2. Hymns of praise then let us sing, al - - - - - - le - lu - ia,

our tri - um - phant ho - ly day, al - - - - - - le - lu - ia,
un - to Christ, our heav'n - ly King, al - - - - - - le - lu - ia,

who did once u - pon the cross, al - - - - - - le - lu - ia,
who en - dured the cross and grave, al - - - - - - le - lu - ia,

suf - fer to re - deem our loss, al - - - - - - le - lu - ia.
sin - ners to re - deem and save, al - - - - - - le - lu - ia.

Descant by Christopher Gower

DESCANT
3. But the pains that he en - dured, al - - - - - - le - lu - ia,
ALL VOICES
3. But the pains that he en - dured, al - - - - - - - - le - lu - ia,
our sal - va - tion have pro - cured, al - - - - - - le - lu - ia,
our sal - va - tion have pro - cured, al - - - - - - le - lu - ia,
now a - bove the sky he's King, al - - - - - le - lu - - - ia,
now a - bove the sky he's King, al - - - - - le - lu - - - ia,

where the an - gels ev - er sing, al - - - - - - le - lu - ia.
where the an - gels ev - er sing, al - - - - - - le - lu - ia.

'Lyra Davidica' 1708

# Judge Eternal, Throned in Splendour

Rhuddlan 87.87.87.

Melody in Edward Jones's
*Musical Relicks of Welsh Bards* 1800

1. Judge et - er - nal throned in splen - dour, Lord of Lords and King of kings,
2. Still the wea - ry folk are pi - ning for the hour that brings re - lease:

with thy liv - ing fire of judge - ment purge this realm of bit - ter things:
and the ci - ty's crowd - ed clan - gour cries a - loud for sin to cease;

so - lace all its wide dom - in - ion with the hea - ling of thy wings.
and the home - steads and the wood - lands plead in si - lence for their peace.

Descant by Christopher Gower
DESCANT
3. Crown, O God, thine own en - dea - vour; cleave the dark - ness with thy sword:
ALL VOICES
3. Crown, O God, thine own en - dea - vour; cleave the dark - ness with thy sword:
feed the faint and hun - gry hea - then with the rich - es of thy word:
feed the faith - less and the hun - gry with the rich - es of thy word:
cleanse the bo - dy of this na - tion through the glo - - - ry of the Lord.
cleanse the bo - dy of this na - tion through the glo - ry of the Lord.

Henry Scott Holland 1874-1918

# Lo! He Comes With Clouds Descending

Helmsley 87.87.47.

Melody noted by T. Olivers 1725-99
Included in Wesley's *Select Hymns* 1765

1. Lo! he ___ comes ___ with ___ clouds ___ de -
2. Ev - 'ry ___ eye ___ shall ___ now ___ be -
3. Those dear ___ to - kens ___ of ___ his ___

scen - ding, once for fa - voured sin - ners ___
hold ___ him robed in dread - ful ma - jes -
pass - ion still his dazz - ling bo - dy ___

slain; ___ thou - sand ___ thou - sand ___ saints ___ at -
ty; ___ those who ___ set ___ at ___ naught ___ and ___
bears, ___ cause of ___ end - less ___ ex - ul -

ten - ding swell the tri - umph of ___ his ___
sold ___ him, pierced and nailed him to ___ the ___
ta - tion to his ran - somed wor - ship -

train: ___ Al - le - lu - ia! Al - le -
tree, ___ deep - ly wail - ing, deep - ly
pers: ___ with ___ what rap - ture, with ___ what

lu - ia! Al - - le - lu - ia!
wail - ing, deep - - ly wail - ing,
rap - ture, with what rap - ture
God ap - pears on earth to reign.
shall the true Mes - si - ah see.
gaze we on those glor - ious scars!

Descant by Christopher Gower
DESCANT
Yea, A - - men! let all ad - ore thee,
ALL VOICES
Yea, A - - men! let all ad - ore thee,
high on thine et - er - nal throne; Sav - iour
high on thine et - er - nal throne; Sav - iour
take the pow'r and glo - ry: claim
take the pow'r and glo - ry: claim the

the King-dom for thine own: O come
King - dom for thine own: O come
quick - ly, O come quick - ly, O come
quick - ly, O come quick - ly, O come
quick - ly, Al - le - lu - ia, Come, Lord, Come.
quick - ly, Al - le - lu - ia, Come, Lord, Come.

Charles Wesley 1707-1788

# Lord, Enthroned in Heav'nly Splendour

St. Helen 87.87.87.

George C Martin 1844-1916

*Unison*

1. Lord, en - throned in heav'n - ly splen - dour, first be - got - ten from the
2. Here our humb - blest hom - age pay we; here in lov - ing re - verence
3. Though the low - liest form doth veil thee as of old in Beth - le -
4. Pas - chal Lamb, thine Offer - ing, fin - ished once for all when thou wast

*Harmony*

dead, thou a - lone, our strong de - fen - der. lift - est up thy peo - ple's
bow; here for faith's dis - cern - ment pray we, lest we fail to know thee
- hem, here as there thine an - gels hail thee, Branch and Flow - er of Jes - se's
slain, in its full - ness un - di - min - ished shall for ev - er - more re -

head. Al - le - lu - ia, al - le - lu - ia, Je - sus, true and liv - ing bread!
now. Al - le - lu - ia, al - le - lu - ia, thou art here, we ask not how.
stem. Al - le - lu - ia, al - le - lu - ia, we in wor - ship join with them.
- main, Al - le - lu - ia, al - le - lu - ia, cleans - ing souls from ev - ery stain.

* *Small notes for organ only*

DESCANT
Descant by Christopher Gower
5. Life - im - par - ting heav' - nly Man - na, strick-en rock with strea - ming
5. Life - im - par - ting heav' - nly Man - na, strick- en rock with strea - ming
side, heav'n and earth with loud hos - an - na wor-ship thee the Lamb who
side, heaven and earth with loud hos - an - na wor - ship thee the Lamb who
died, Al - le - lu - ia, al - le - lu - ia, ris'n, asc-end - ed, glo - ri - fied.
died, Al - le - lu - ia, al - le - lu - ia, risen, asc - end - ed, glo - ri - fied.

G. H. Bourne 1840-1925

# Love's Redeeming Work is Done

Savannah (Hermhut) 77.77.

Melody from MS. *Choralbuch*
Hermhut c. 1740 as given in
J. Wesley's *Foundery Collection* 1742

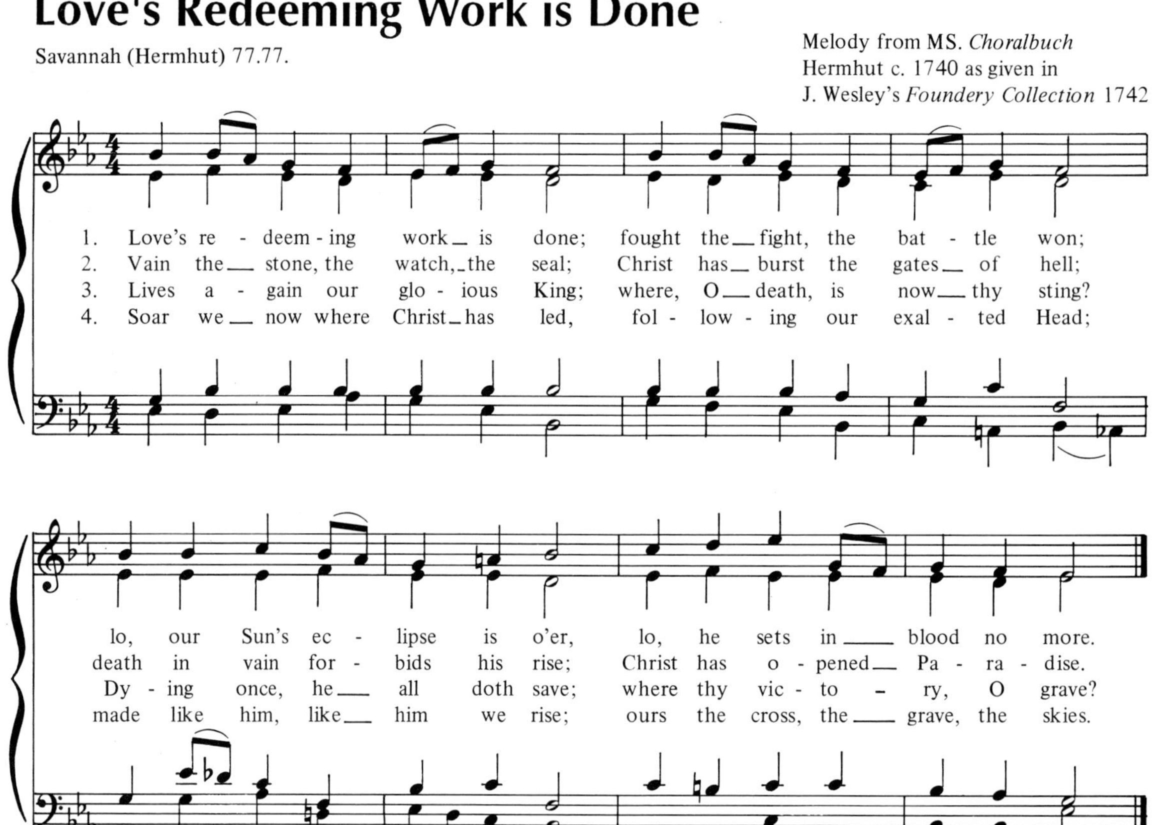

1. Love's re - deem - ing work — is done; fought the — fight, the bat - tle won;
2. Vain the — stone, the watch, — the seal; Christ has — burst the gates — of hell;
3. Lives a - gain our glo - ious King; where, O — death, is now — thy sting?
4. Soar we — now where Christ — has led, fol - low - ing our exal - ted Head;
lo, our Sun's ec - lipse is o'er, lo, he sets in — blood no more.
death in vain for - bids his rise; Christ has o - pened — Pa - ra - dise.
Dy - ing once, he — all doth save; where thy vic - to - ry, O grave?
made like him, like — him we rise; ours the cross, the — grave, the skies.

Descant by Christopher Gower

DESCANT
5. Hail the Lord of earth and heav'n! Praise — to thee by both be — giv'n: thee — we greet tri - um - phant now; hail the res - ur - rec - tion thou!
ALL VOICES
5. Hail the — Lord of earth — and heaven! Praise to — thee by thee — be given: thee we greet tri - um - phant now; hail the res - ur - rec - tion thou!

Charles Wesley 1707-1788

# Now Thank We All Our God

Nundanket 67.67.66.66.

Melody in J. Cruger's
*Praxis Pietatis Melica* c. 1647
Harmony chiefly from Mendelssohn's *Lobgesang* 1840

1. Now thank we all our God, with heart and hands and voic - es, who
2. O may this bount - eous God through all our life be near us, with
won - drous things hath done, in whom his world re - joic - es; who
ev - er joy - ful hearts and bless - ed peace to cheer us; and
from our moth - er's arms hath blessed — us on our way with
keep us in his grace, and guide — us when per - plexed, and
count - less gifts of love, and still is ours to - day.
free us from all ills in this world and the next

Descant by Christopher Gower

DESCANT
3. All praise_ and_ thanks to God___, the Fa - ther now be_ giv - en,
ALL VOICES
3. All praise and thanks to God, the Fa - ther now be giv - en, the
the Son,and him who reigns ___ with_them in high - est heav'n,
Son, and him who reigns with them in high - est hea - ven, the
the One_ et - er - nal God, Whom earth_ and heav'n ad - ore:___
One et - er - nal God, Whom earth_ and heav'n ad - ore: for

for thus it was, is now, and shall be ev - er - more.
thus it was, is now, and shall be ev - er - more.

German, Martin Rinkart 1586-1649
Tr. Catherine Winkworth 1827-1878

# O God, Our Help in Ages Past

St. Anne CM.

Melody and bass from
*A supplement to the New Version* 1708,
probably supplied by William Croft 1678-1727

1. O God, our help in ages past, our hope for years to come, our shelter from the stormy blast, and our eternal home.
2. Beneath the shadow of thy throne, thy saints have dwelt secure; sufficient is thine arm alone, and our defence is sure.
3. Before the hills in order stood, or earth received her frame, from everlasting thou art God, to endless years the same.
4. A thousand ages in thy sight, are like an evening gone; short as the watch that ends the night before the rising sun.
5. Time, like an ever-rolling stream, bears all its sons away; they fly forgotten, as a dream dies at the opening day.

Descant by Christopher Gower
DESCANT
6. O God, our help in a - ges past, our hope for
ALL VOICES
6. O God, our help in a - ges past, our hope for years to
years to come, be thou our guide while trou - bles last, and our e-ter-nal home.
come, be thou our guide while trou-bles last, and our e - ter - nal home.

Isaac Watts 1674-1748

# Ride On! Ride On in Majesty

Winchester New LM.

Adapted from a chorale in *Musicalisches Hand-Buch,* Hamburg, 1690

1. Ride on! Ride on in maj - es - ty! Hark, all the tribes ho - san - na cry: thy hum - ble beast pur - sues his road with palms and scat - tered gar - ments strowed.
2. Ride on! Ride on in maj - es - ty! In low - ly pomp ride on to die: O Christ, thy tri - umphs now be - gin o'er cap - tive death and con - quered sin.
3. Ride on! Ride on in maj - es - ty! The wing - ed sqad - rons of the sky look down with sad and wond - ering eyes to see the approach - ing sac - ri - fice.
4. Ride on! Ride on in maj - es - ty! Thy last and fierc - est strife is nigh; the Fa - ther, on his sap - phire throne, ex - pects his own an - oint - ed Son.

Descant by Christopher Gower

DESCANT
5. Ride on! Ride on in maj - es - ty! Ride
ALL VOICES
5. Ride on! Ride on in maj - es - ty! in low - ly pomp ride
on to die; bow thy head to mor - tal pain,
on to die; bow thy meek head to mor - tal pain, then
take, O God, the power, and reign.
take, O God, thy power, and reign.

Henry Milman 1791-1868

# Stand Up and Bless the Lord

Carlisle SM.

Charles Lockhart (1745-1815)

1. Stand up and bless the Lord, ye peo - ple of his choice; stand
2. Though high a - bove all praise, a - bove all bless - ing high, who
3. O for the liv - ing flame from his own al - tar brought, to
4. God is our strength and song, and his sal - va - tion ours; then

up, and bless the Lord your God with heart and soul and voice.
would not fear his ho - ly name, and laud and mag - ni - fy?
touch our lips, our mind in - spire, and wing to heaven our thought.
be his love in Christ pro - claimed with all our ran - somed powers.

Descant by Christopher Gower
DESCANT
5. Stand up, and bless the Lord, the Lord your God ad - ore; Stand up, and bless his glo - rious name hence - forth for ev - er - more.
ALL VOICES
5. Stand up, and bless the Lord, the Lord your God ad - ore; Stand up, and bless his glo - rious name hence - forth for ev - er - more.

James Montgomery 1771-1854

# The day thou gavest, Lord, is ended

St. Clement 98.98. Charles C. Scholefield 1839-1904

1. The day thou ga - vest, Lord, is end - ed, the dark - ness falls at thy be - hest; to thee our morn - ing hymns as - cen - ded, thy praise shall sanc - ti - fy our rest.
2. We thank thee that the Church un - sleep - ing, while earth rolls on - ward in - to light, through all the world her watch is keep - ing, and rests not now by day or night.
3. As o'er each con - tin - ent and isl - and the dawn leads on an - oth - er day, the voice of prayer is nev - er si - lent, nor dies the strain of praise a - way.
4. The sun that bids us rest is wa - king our breth - ren 'neath the west - ern sky, and hour by hour fresh lips are ma - king thy won - drous do - ings heard on high.

Descant by Christopher Gower
DESCANT
5. So be it, Lord; thy throne shall ne - ver, like
ALL VOICES
5. So be it, Lord; thy throne shall ne - ver, like earth's proud
earth's proud em - pire pass aw - ay; thy king - dom stands and
em - pire, pass aw - ay; thy king - dom stands and
grows for ev - er, till thy crea - tures own thy sway.
grows for ev - er, till all thy crea - tures own thy sway.

John Ellerton 1826-1893

# The God of Abraham praise

Leoni 66.84.D

Hebrew melody noted by T. Olivers 1725-99
from the singing of Meyer Lyon of the
London Great Synagogue. Adapted c. 1770

1. The God of A - braham praise who reigns en - throned a - bove, an -
2. Though na - ture's strength de - cay, and earth and hell with - stand, to
3. The good - ly land we see, with peace and plen - ty blest: a
4. There dwells the Lord our King, the Lord of right - eous - ness, tri -
5. Be - fore the great Three - One they all ex - ult - ing stand, and
6. The God who reigns on high the great arch - an - gels sing, and
7. Be - fore the Sa - viour's face the ran - somed na - tions bow, o'er -
cient of e - ver - last - ing days and God of love; to
Ca - naan's bounds we urge our way at his com - mand: the
land of sa - cred li - ber - ty and end - less rest; there
um - phant o'er the world of sin, the Prince of peace; on
tell the won - ders he hath done through all their land: the
Ho - ly, Ho - ly, Ho - ly,' cry, 'al - migh - ty King! who
whelmed at his al - migh - ty grace for e - ver new; he
him up - lift your voice, at whose su - preme com - mand from
wa - tery deep we pass, with Je - sus in our view; and
milk and ho - ney flow, and oil and wine a - bound, and
Zi - on's sa - cred height his king - dom he main - tains, and
list - ening spheres at - tend, and swell the grow - ing fame, and
was, and is the same, and e - ver - more shall be; e -
shows his prints of love they kin - dle to a flame, and

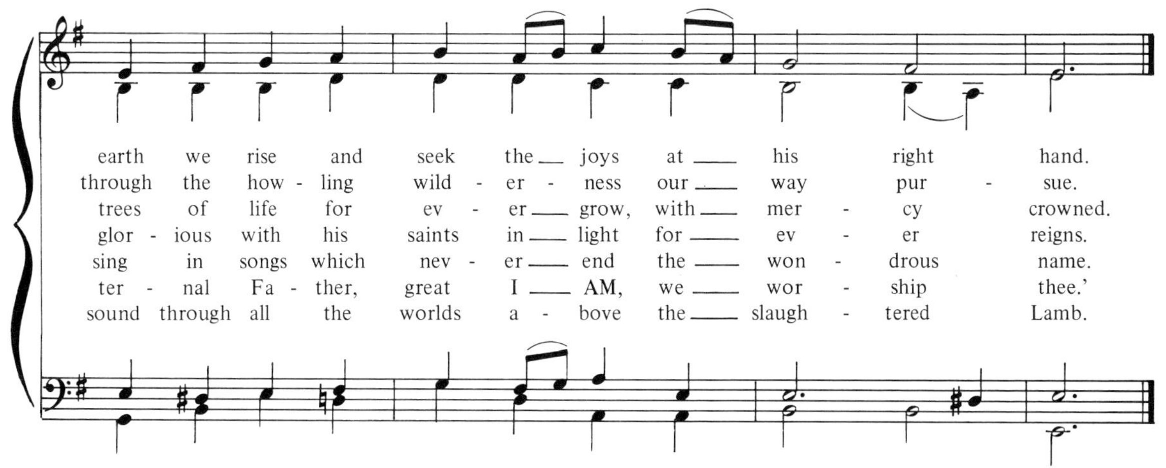
earth we rise and seek the joys at his right hand.
through the how - ling wild - er - ness our way pur - sue.
trees of life for ev - er grow, with mer - cy crowned.
glor - ious with his saints in light for ev - er reigns.
sing in songs which nev - er end the won - drous name.
ter - nal Fa - ther, great I AM, we wor - ship thee.'
sound through all the worlds a - bove the slaugh - tered Lamb.

Descant by Christopher Gower

DESCANT
8. The whole tri - um - phant host give thanks to God on high; 'hail
ALL VOICES
8. The whole tri - um - phant host give thanks to God on high; 'hail
Fa - ther, Son, and Ho - ly Ghost', they ev - - - - - - er cry. Hail, Ab - r'am's
Fa - ther, Son, and Ho - ly Ghost', they ev - er cry. Hail,
God and mine, (I join the hea - - v'nly lays) all
Ab - raham's God and mine, (I join the heav - enly lays) all

might and maj - est - ty are thine, and end - less praise.
might and maj - est - ty are thine, and end - less praise.

Thomas Olivers 1725-99
based on the Hebrew *Yigdal*

# To the Name that Brings Salvation

Oriel 87.87.87.

Tune as set to *Pange lingua* in
C. Ett's *Cantica Sacra* Munich 1840

1. To the name that brings sal - va - tion ho - nour, wor - ship, laud we pray:
2. Name of glad - ness, name of plea - sure, by the tongue in - eff - ab - ble,
3. 'Tis the name for a - dor - a - tion, 'tis the name of vic - tor - y;
4. 'Tis the name that who - so preach - es finds it mu - sic in his ear;
5. 'Tis the name by right ex - al - ted o - ver ev - ery oth - er name:
6. Je - su, we thy name a - dor - ing, long to see thee as thou art:

that for many a gen - er - a - tion hid in God's fore - know - ledge lay,
name of sweet - ness, pass - ing mea - sure, to the ear de - lect - ab - le;
'tis the name for me - di - ta - tion in the vale of mis - er - y:
'tis the name that who - so teach - es finds more sweet than hon - ey's cheer:
that when we are sore as - sul - ted puts our en - e - mies to shame:
of thy clem - en - cy im - plor - ing so to write it in our heart,

but to e -very tongue and na - tion Ho - ly Church pro - claims to - day.
'tis our safe - guard and our trea - sure, 'tis our help 'gainst sin and hell.
'tis the name for ven - er - a - tion by the ci - ti - zens on high.
who its per - fect wis - dom reach - es makes his ghost - ly vi - sion clear.
strength to them that else had halt - ed, eyes to blind, and feet to lame.
that here - af - ter, up - ward soar - ing, we with an - gels may have part.

DESCANT
Descant by Christopher Gower
7. Where thou reign - est with the Fa - ther, thou the e - ver - last - ing Son,
ALL VOICES
7. Where thou reign - est with the Fa - ther, thou the e - ver - last - ing Son,
Where with the e - ter - nal Spi - rit three - fold God, yet e - ver One, May
Where with the e - ter - nal Spi - rit three - fold God, yet e - ver One.
our eyes be - hold the splend - our when our earth - ly course is done.
May our eyes be - hold the splend - our when our earth - ly course is done.

Latin c. 15th century. Tr. J.M.Neale

# Ye Holy Angels Bright

Darwall's 148th. 66.66.44.44. John Darwall 1731-89

1. Ye ho - ly an - gels bright, who wait at God's right hand, or
2. Ye bless - ed souls at rest, who ran this earth - ly race. and
3. Ye saints, who toil be - low, a - dore your heaven- ly King, and
through the realms of light fly at your Lord's com - mand, as - sist our
now, from sin re - leased, be - hold the Sav - iour's face. his prais - es,
on - ward as ye go some joy - ful an - them sing; take what he
song, for else the theme too high doth seem for mor - tal tongue.
sound, as in his light with sweet de - light ye do a - bound.
gives and praise him still, through good or ill, who ev - er lives.

Descant by Christopher Gower
DESCANT
4. My soul, bear thou thy part, tri - umph in God ab-ove,
ALL VOICES
4. My soul, bear thou thy part, tri - umph in God ab - ove, and
and with a well-tuned heart sing thou the songs of love; let all thy days,
with a well - tuned heart sing thou the songs of love; let all thy
let all thy days till life shall end what - 'er he send be filled with praise.
days till life shall end, what - 'er he send be filled with praise.

Richard Baxter 1615-1691